*This is exactly what I would tell people about my own recovery from depression. I'm grateful for Linda's ability to clarify and give courage, compassion, and connection to guide us in this process.*

—Shem Watson, Advocate for mental wellness and recovery

Quiet Mind *embraces all the ingredients for recovery from mental struggle. I loved Linda's realness, honesty, and integrity. Her words are filled with wisdom and reflect her own effort to move into this brilliant and clear space. You will find yourself on a powerful path to recovery. Excellent!*

—Meredith Young-Sowers, D. Div., Co-founder of the Stillpoint Foundation

*Linda speaks from her experience with the devastating lows of illness and depression. In* Quiet Mind, *she shares the tips and tools she used to create medication-free health and wellness. Her  style is compassionate, humorous and that of a knowledgeable mentor gently encouraging readers to find their path.*

—Dr. Ruth Anderson, Founder of
Enlightened World

*I have been working in the field of mental health recovery for over thirty years and have improved my life and those of others using the course corrections that Linda has encapsulated into this useful handbook. I will recommend it to my friends, my supporters, and to people who reach out to me for guidance.*

—Mary Ellen Copeland, Founder of the
Copeland Center for Wellness and Recovery

*I am wowed by the depth of knowledge and know-how that Linda has compiled into this mini-book—a roadmap toward empowerment and wellbeing from anxiety and depression. Linda encourages us to find our growth and to cheer each other on as we move to joy and wellness.*

—Dido Clark, Ph.D., Blogger, web content creator, and editor, www.expressably.com

# Quiet Mind

## How to Create Freedom from Depression and Anxiety

## Linda Dierks

Quiet Mind: How to Create Freedom from Depression and
Anxiety
Published by Spin Straw to Gold
Palm Springs, CA

www.SpinStrawtoGoldNow.com

ISBN: 978-1-0916970-6-5

Psychopathology / Depression

# Dedication

This book is for anyone
who wants more joy in life.
I dedicate it to you for taking
this first step.

# Introduction

I'm a mental health insider. Full disclosure: In my mid-forties, after years of intermittent depression and suspected mood swings, I sought professional help and was diagnosed with Bipolar II, the lesser of mood-swing evils. I was told that my condition could be controlled with medication but that I would never be cured. I've never liked or accepted the words "can't" or "forever," and kept looking for a solution. Then, a decade later when breast cancer left me debilitated and depressed, finding the source of emotional wellness became my life's mission.

People like you and me have known the dark times of living in the scorching cauldron of despair, hope-lessness, fear, self-doubt, and injustice. The despair of emotional torture. The hopelessness of believing this is all life will ever be. The fear of knowing you are out of control. The fear of the effect your symptoms will have on your relationships and your job. The fear of being discovered and losing your credibility. The self-doubt, and not trusting your brain or yourself. The injustice behind "why me?" The wasted potential, or living a life that seems more like a punishment than a blessing.

But my years of research paid off and I am one of the few who—plunged into the conventional mental healthcare system—emerged victorious from depression and anxiety by designing my own wellness program, *Quiet Mind*. I've been symptom-free and medication-free for more than seven years and I'm proof of this program's success. I'm the messenger of these fundamental truths and gladly take on this role to save others from the unnecessary suffering I went through. It truly is my passion to share my success with you. This is your time to regain your power and your inner flame of strength and joy.

This simple program provides the education, tools, and practices to achieve success and ignite your world. It's your chance to become your genuine self and come out from behind the curtain of mental turmoil. You can create a life you only dreamed of until now. Your natural vibrancy can shine, and your footing can be unshakable. The transformation is subtle, consistent, and constantly unfolding. For me, it has created a new sense of bound-less freedom and joy. This can be yours too.

Together we'll step onto a healthier path to emo-tional health that can reduce and even eliminate pre-scription medications. Intrigued? Maybe, like me, you want the power to create your own wellness. You may not be getting satisfactory relief from your existing course or are fed up with chemical treatments. Or you know there's a source of wellness that can be accessed via a path of wholeness and based in higher awareness. You might be asking:

▷ *There's so much out there; where do I start?*

▷ *What's going to be most effective?*

▷ *Is it difficult to incorporate into my lifestyle?*

▷ *If there are effective, non-traditional practices, why don't we all know about them?*

Do you wish someone would wade through all of this and put you on the fast-track? Well, I did just that! For more than a decade, I turned over every stone,

researched leading-edge practices, simplified the language, tested each method, discarded procedures
too burdensome to incorporate, pulled out the most
effective gems, and bundled them into this clear and
streamlined mini-handbook.

## Finally, a proven solution
## to depression and anxiety.

Mastering my mental health challenges is my
proudest accomplishment and has yielded a cornuco-
pia of skills and benefits around higher awareness that
continue to create more pleasure and success for me.
If you also face emotional challenges, I feel a kinship
with you. A full and rewarding life is waiting for you.
Together, we'll achieve it.

# History

The mystery around the functioning of our brains creates a "throw a dart at the board" approach to depression and anxiety treatment. I don't fault the industry. I know my doctors were doing their best with the tools they'd been taught. But the tools at their disposal were based on trial-and-error and limited to the confines of the insurance industry. I repeatedly heard the line, "Well, let's try this and see what happens," which sounded suspiciously like a throwback from the '60s. At the time, prescription treatment was little more than an educated guess, and I was another guinea pig. Have you felt this way as well?

Was this the best I could hope for? Did I have to accept that the rest of my life would look this way? What relief I gained from my symptoms was a lousy trade-off to the side effects of weight gain, blur-ry-headedness, constipation or diarrhea, hand trem-ors, and a feeling that I wasn't in control of my life. One drug caused me to behave erratically; another affected my heart so severely I barely made it home from a simple walk. My brain was always in a chem-ical cloud and I missed that clear "ping" that brings inspiration and creative thought.

**The relief I gained from drugs was marginal.**
**Drugs may dull your symptoms**
**but make you feel numb and clouded.**

Like me, have you been asking yourself if the side effects are worth it? Some studies indicate that anti-depressants have only a negligible advantage over placebos. People can and do get physically addicted to their medications, but worse still, they can become emotionally addicted, as fear about living without their meds gets an iron grip. Medication becomes part of the problem, not the solution. My meds caused me a host of problems, but the last straw for me was that they stole my sex life. I found myself saying, "Enough of the meds!" I knew there had to be a better route. I shifted my beliefs and mustered my courage, knowing there was a better solution and that I would find it.

My transformation emerged from what I call my "Dark Ages." In only a few short years, I had developed cancer and escalating depression. I lost my job, my identity, my sanity, all my money, and my right breast. Overwhelmed by fear and with a nervous system pushed beyond its limits, I was beyond the reach of conventional medicine. I was forced to take a broader view of healing and trust that wellness could rest in my own hands. I began a meditation practice that released my trauma and restored the stillness that nurtures healing. After exploring advanced wellness concepts, I learned that I could create a healthy and vibrant healing environment by guiding my thoughts and attitudes to create calm and attract positive energy.

It began with small changes as I started editing out anything that created tension or conflict. I chose to let go of being judgmental, critical, or controlling, focusing instead on appreciation, harmony, and love. With these practices, I was on my way to restructuring my brain and changing the patterns that were contributing to my emotional instability. I replaced old patterns and triggers with a new roadmap to natural peace and emotional resilience. I became stronger, more confident, and less reactive to fears and petty annoyances. All this created a new stillness in my life. Establishing a solid meditation and mind-management practice was the foundation on which I'd build my future success. There is no mental illness in the presence of a quiet mind.

Then, through one of life's synchronistic coincidences, I met Dr. Lewis Mehl-Madrona, a talented psychiatrist and psychologist with a background in alternative healing that stemmed from his roots in Native American culture. He introduced me to a natural mental health nutritional supplement program called Truehope. The program's free counselors gradually weaned me off prescription medications and onto their natural treatment program. After fifteen years and twelve different drugs, I was free!

Nothing will make you doubt yourself more than a brain you can't trust. You, too, may have found yourself sinking into a deep sadness that you know is not real, but you can't see beyond the hopelessness of it. Or perhaps you feel like you are being thrashed by an anxious brain that's racing out of control and you're powerless to stop it. Sound familiar?

I assure you that there is a kinder and simpler way

out. After my success, I wrote to Dr. Mehl-Madrona and said, "My depression issues had sapped me of my confidence. I was always doubting myself, and I was terrified of the stigma—that people would find out. It robbed me of my identity, never knowing what was "me" and what was my faulty brain. It eroded my self-worth, always thinking that I was damaged and less than everyone else. I never dreamed I could feel this whole and talented—what an extraordinary gift you have given me." My light was no longer under a bushel.

I won't claim it was a bed of roses. I, too, had become physically and psychologically reliant on the drugs and I had to tough it out through some challenging times. But the reward was enormous. This weaning process would have been easier if I hadn't been so fearful, so I confidently assure you that you can follow this route to wellness and also succeed. The progress is gradual but yields undreamed-of rewards.

My brain came back to a clear, joyful state—enriched, curious, and receptive. My body and mind were cleansed of toxins. The Truehope program helped eliminate my symptoms, freed me from the cloud of chemicals and cleared the lingering mental haze I'd experienced since chemotherapy. I was more receptive, curious, mentally agile, and smarter—all self-directed and free of harmful drugs. You have to do the work, but the outcome can be a miracle.

# Introducing the
# Quiet Mind Program

Modern mental health treatments focus on re-shaping how our thoughts and attitudes imprint our brains, or in psych-talk: cognitive thought, de-conditioning, and neuro-linguistic programming. Applying the tools of the *Quiet Mind* approach achieves the same result but with the simpler language of quieting the mind and managing your inner dialogue. These methods replace structured protocols and harsh drugs, are easy to incorporate, gentler, and more effective. And because you're targeting the conditions of depression and anxiety, not just the symptoms, you can achieve long-lasting results.

Scientists agree that mental illness is the result

of faulty communication between neurons and low levels of serotonin in the brain. By incorporating these tools, you can subtly re-wire these neurons in a process known as neuroplasticity or brain sculpting, and naturally raise serotonin levels, correcting your brain's chemistry.

Join me. I'll show you how with these four sets of tools. Let's start with the first set, designed to help bring about a calm mind.

## 1. Calm Mind

From a state of calm, you can release stress, fear, anger, and trauma. This place of stillness is the fertile ground where your natural joy and well-being can prosper. It puts you in a higher frequency and is your connection to the spark of the divine that can never be tarnished by illness. When in peace, your brain becomes pliable and more receptive to new changes. This is the foundation on which you can create a calm and unshakable core.

> ▷ **Create a quiet mind**—Meditation is the most effective means of stilling the mind. Other practices include counting your breath, drumming,

chanting, praying (with rosaries if that speaks to you), mindfulness, using mantras, or having quiet time in nature. Anything that gets the brain out of the way is beneficial.

What appeals most to you? You'll be more committed to your practice if you find something you enjoy. But working toward a proficient and committed meditation practice will bring you the greatest results. Clinical studies indicate that mindfulness-based interventions are generally as effective as antidepressants. Meditation is easily learned with practice and consistency or by taking classes in person, using phone apps, or taking classes online.

▷ **Control stress**—Prioritize your health above all else. Commit to sensible choices in your activities, your career, and your relationships. Stress produces the dense, low-vibration energy that accompanies depression, stifles physical and mental vitality, and keeps you locked in reactive and harmful patterns.

▷ **Nurture a spiritual practice**—A connection with something greater than yourself anchors you and minimizes life's calamities. Regardless of your definition of a higher presence, make that force a friend, a coach, your comfort in rough times, and a presence that is always committed to your greatest good.

You may be fortunate to live in a community that hosts a Center for Spiritual Living that teaches productive thought. Other open-thought communities include the Unitarian Universalist, Unity, and Quaker churches. Perhaps a more traditional religion may appeal to you. Spiritual communities can lift your mood, alleviate the isolation that often accompanies depression, and offer opportunities to be of service. All these will help raise your serotonin levels.

## My Action Notes

_____

_____

_____

_____

_____

_____

_____

_____

_____

_____

## 2. Inner Dialogue

Your inner dialogue includes your thoughts, attitudes, beliefs, emotions, reactions, and self-esteem. Negative thinking and pessimism generate emotional imbalance and can become a constant habit. Your inner environment will always become your physical reality. When you cultivate positive, uplifting mind management, you nourish your brain and restore balance. Every decision you make, every thought you think, every word you speak, every attitude you express, is either hurting or helping you. The more skilled you become, the more your life spirals upward. Glowing health is only a pivot of thought away.

▷ **Thought management**—Negative or toxic thinking is a major cause of stress and generates the dense energy around depression. Examine your ingrained habits and old patterns and ask yourself, "Is this thought serving me? Is this attitude enriching my health and well-being?" Turn off your auto-pilot and be conscious of what you feed your brain. Swap unconstructive attitudes for nurturing thoughts. Live in positive expectancy, reach for the higher thought, and seek the kinder conclusion. Create a thoughtmosphere that gives rise to a vibrant mood.

▷ **Attitudes and beliefs**—Your attitudes and beliefs are reflected in your mental health. Often these have been deeply programmed into your subconscious by years of repetition. As you re-train your brain, you gradually change your neuropathways, steering thoughts away from harmful patterns and into healthier attitudes that take the edge off life. Ask yourself, "Is this attitude serving my highest good?" "Are my beliefs wholesome and in alignment with the way I live my life?" You have to walk the walk as well as talk the talk. Negative frames of mind are only learned behaviors that can be un-learned.

▷ **Emotions and reactions**—Soften your emotions and reactions, and you can calm your brain. Be aware of how you react to external stimuli and the depth to which you experience them. Are you able to be an observer and allow stress, personal injustices, and trauma to pass through you or do you dwell on and "awfulize" each event?

This doesn't mean you should suppress your feelings—it means to react in a way that doesn't harm you. By taking out the drama and electricity, you avoid imprinting your brain with abrasive and injurious stimuli.

▷ **Self-esteem**—People out of harmony with themselves are prone to depression and anxiety. Creating a quiet mind begins with how you treat yourself. Outward self-esteem is the result of a positive inner dialogue. When you exercise self-compassion and release self-judgment, you can become your best coach and cheerleader. Self-esteem comes from being authentic, standing in your truth, and finding your unique gifts. Every time you look in the mirror, smile at yourself and say, "I love you."

## My Action Notes

_____

_____

_____

_____

_____

_____

_____

_____

_____

_____

## 3. Lifestyle Practices

Modern lifestyles include rampant urbanization that takes us away from our natural environment. Electronic devices subject us to electromagnetic pollution, promote isolation, and sedentary lifestyles. These leave our energy dense and clogged. Live your life in a way that anchors, reinforces, and increases the success of your Quiet Mind practices. Here are the most important lifestyle practices that I have found:

▷ **Physical exercise**—Regular exercise has been shown to be more effective than pills by releasing endorphins, taking the mind off stress, and keeping energy systems flowing. Simple walking also creates cross-patterning that boosts cognitive thought, balances the left and right hemispheres of the brain, and reorganizes your mind-body connections. Yoga and stretching release stress stored in your cells, increase vitality, and trigger the body's natural healing ability. Vibrant body, vibrant mind.

▷ **Get out in nature**—City dwelling is associated with increased levels of mental illness. Nature calms and produces endorphins, relaxes the psyche, and promotes freshness and renewal. In nature, you reinforce your connection to a higher presence and become part of a greater whole.

▷ **Get out of the house**—Distractions can take your focus away from your issues and prevent you from ruminating. Solitude is the breeding ground of depression. Go out for coffee, window shop, or spend face-to-face time with friends and social groups. Get to know your neighbors. Surround yourself with people who are energetic and cheerful. Network with others who experience mental health symptoms to share ideas and lift the stigma.

▷ **Avoid substances that affect your brain**—Drugs, nicotine, even coffee, and especially alcohol, affect your brain. Caffeine will intensify anxiety. It wasn't until I backed away from alcohol that I realized how much its residual effect exacerbated my insomnia, depression, and anxiety, creating a self-perpetuating cycle. The brain can self-balance if you quit aggravating it. Resist the urge to self-medicate.

▷ **Live in an attitude of love**—Living from the heart is more powerful, wiser, and gentler than living from the brain and helps reshape those neuropathways. A heart-centered focus boosts your self-esteem, generates wiser choices, and diminishes negative emotional reactions. Love is the highest frequency and the presence of the divine in your life.

▷ **Visualize**—Remember what it felt like to be happy. Replay it, relive it, repeat. Picture the person you want to be and avoid a persona of victimhood or woundedness. Express gratitude for your steady improvement, and in doing so, you can "glue" that energy to you. An ounce of visualization is worth a pound of effort.

▷ **Affirmations**—Repeating affirmations is an effective way to access your subconscious and implement healthier thoughts and behaviors. As a visual reminder, put your affirmations on sticky notes, post them in prominent places, and swap them out regularly. Create your own or start with:

- "I am perfect, whole, and complete."

- "I am radiant when I radiate love."

- "Calm encircles my mind and body."

- "I am compassionate and gentle with myself."

- "I experience great delight in my life."

▷ **Professional counseling**—Establish a rapport with a licensed professional to pull you out of the rut of stinkin' thinkin' and steer you toward constructive ways of viewing and coping with the world. My skilled counselor helped me manage my downtimes, set higher sights for myself, and achieve maximum learning and growth from my experiences.

▷ **Electronics**: Ouch. Where to begin?

- **Social media**—Spending time on social media is reported to increase self-doubt and lower self-esteem by promoting unhealthy comparisons and a fear of missing out (known as FOMO). Social media programs are intentionally designed to entrap participants through a "dopamine loop," and are suspected of making teens more vulnerable to addictions. Limiting social media to thirty minutes or less per day has been shown to significantly decrease depression, anxiety, and loneliness.

• **Electronic communication**—Manage your attention by minimizing interruptions and annoyances. Managing your attention increases your state of calm and reinforces patience. Perhaps you can't resist the temptation to respond to those rings and beeps, even though they put you in a reactive vs. a proactive mindset. A reactive mindset will only disrupt your focus, generate anxiety, and can cause attention deficit disorder (ADD). Discourage those around you from texting you in favor of less intrusive e-mailing, and respond to messages on your time, not someone else's. When you limit interruptions from the outer world, you grow your inner world.

• **Television, movies, and news**—Avoid violence and high suspense—you can't watch it without being part of the toxic energy. Negative and sensationalized news reinforces chaos and generates anxiety, anger, and disgust. Switch from negative news to healthier, more positive programming. I subscribe to The Optimist Daily (www.optimistdaily.com) for upbeat daily news about health, the environment, and personal development.

- **Electromagnetic frequency exposure**—The low-frequency electromagnetic toxicity of your devices generates widespread neuropsychiatric effects, including anxiousness, depression, stress, and fatigue. Keep your cell phone at least five feet away, especially when sleeping. Swap your Wi-Fi for an ethernet cable. Insomnia problems? The blue light emitted by your computer, phone, tablet, and TV suppresses the production of melatonin that promotes sleep. Disconnect from your devices at least an hour before bedtime.

- **Constant availability**—How "on stage" do you really want to be to the outside world? Take a technology vacation and get refreshingly disconnected. Make electronics a tool you use, not a tool that uses you. New reports indicate that the gizmo craze is fading; people are recognizing the value of reconnecting to themselves and others and craving the peace of being free from interruptions. Flip phones are resurging in popularity. Turn your phone off and create extended times when you are device-free. When you're connected, you're not connected. When you're connected to electronics, you're not connected to a higher source.

## My Action Notes

_____

_____

_____

_____

_____

_____

_____

_____

_____

_____

## 4. Natural Remedies

Treating your symptoms with natural nutrition and alternative health modalities can be equally as effective as medication. THIS approach is non-invasive, eliminates side effects, puts you in control, and can be used for extended periods without losing its effectiveness. The contribution of natural remedies was key to my success.

▷ **Truehope**—The Truehope nutritional supplement program has an outstanding track record of relieving symptoms. Use it to boost your existing treatment regimen or rid yourself of drugs entirely. Their free counselors work with you to provide motivation, expertise, and support as you wean yourself off prescription drugs. Once I began sharing my Truehope success with others, I discovered the program's success was already widely known in the mental health underground—another example of the importance of sharing with each other.

▷ **Vitamin D**—Large doses of vitamin D can ease depression symptoms. Take 20,000 mg. spread throughout the day.

▷ **Inositol**—Adding inositol powder calms the mind. Take one-fourth teaspoon four times daily. I pre-mix pitchers of water and drink it during the day.

▷ **Choline**—Choline quiets the body and mind when weaning from prescription medications, and improves memory. Take 2,000 mg spread over the day.

▷ **Amino acids**—Amino acids are the building blocks of life. They calm the brain and body, aid with sleep, and ease withdrawal from chemical meds. Take as your brand directs.

▷ **Magnesium**—Studies indicate that taking 2,000 mg per day cuts depression by more than half. It also serves as a muscle and nervous system relaxant and relieves constipation. Natural Calm, a high-magnesium powder, makes a great bedtime drink that promotes sleep and regularity.

▷ **Acetyl-L-carnitine**—People with low levels of ALC have more serious symptoms of stress and anxiety and are more likely to develop depression later in life. The recommended dosage is 500 mg, four times a day.

▷ **Naturopathic modalities**—Naturopathic modalities are non-invasive, non-toxic, and treat the underlying cause of the imbalance, not just the symptoms. A naturopathic doctor provides healthier alternatives to pharmaceuticals, especially for blood pressure, acid reflux, and rheumatoid arthritis medications that can cause depression. Also, the more prescription drugs you take, the higher your risk of emotional imbalance.

▷ **Gut biome**—Your gut produces 65 percent of your serotonin. Balance your gut with probiotics and two tablespoons of apple cider vinegar in a glass of water, twice daily.

▷ **Medical marijuana CBD oil**—CBD oil is gaining recognition as a new "miracle" drug that can help combat anxiety, panic attacks, insomnia, and inflammation.

▷ **Acupuncture, reiki, and Jin Shin Jyutsu**—Alternative healing modalities stimulate energy flow and balance, relax and relieve stress, and help relieve the heavy, dense feeling that accompanies depression. Acupuncture provided me with rapid relief from my symptoms.

▷ **Chiropractic treatment**—A chiropractic adjustment releases serotonin and endorphins, elevating mood and reducing stress. It also removes energetic blockages, increases vitality, and is more cost-effective than uninsured alternative treatments.

▷ **Light therapy**—Winter's shorter, darker days can stimulate excess secretion of daytime melatonin, sometimes triggering seasonal affective disorder (SAD). Replace your light bulbs with full-spectrum light or use a full-spectrum light box or visor for ten to twenty minutes each morning. I found the visor more convenient. Also, walk in natural light, without your eyeglasses, if possible.

▷ **Diet**—Depression thrives on sweets. Avoid sugar, which includes alcohol and processed foods. Choose leafy greens, vegetables, fruits, and nuts. Fish and olive oil are also rich in helpful Omega 3s.

For general maintenance, I take amino acids, inositol, and magnesium for calming, and a minimum dose of Truehope Empower Plus to keep my brain sharp. Empower Plus, amino acids, probiotics, choline, and inositol, are available at www.truehope.com. Their prices may be more competitive than those of others and they offer financial aid.

## My Action Notes

# Building Your New Life

There is no secret code or fast-track. It's your personal pact of practice, persistence, and patience. It's the process of stacking one habit on top of another and making gradual changes one choice at a time. If your mood takes a dip, just revisit these pages. Approach this path with a peaceful mind and generous heart. Be gentle and compassionate with yourself. But be more tomorrow than you are today.

Haven't you always known there's more for you? Pause. Form a picture in your mind of the life you desire. Visualize and claim it as yours. Then cement it to you with belief and positive expectancy. Emotional turmoil can be a thing of the past. Living in a cloud of uncertainty and self-doubt can become a fading memory. Your habits of worry, stress, anger, and frustration will fade. Your natural state of joy, positivity, and peace will return.

And these practices and skills don't apply only to mental health. The *Quiet Mind* approach will also be your roadmap to vibrant physical health, help you combat addictions, and create higher awareness. All of this happened for me.

## As you move up the emotional ladder, you will raise your consciousness and your life can shift.

You'll begin to engage with the world with a higher perspective that produces happier relationships, a naturally positive outlook, greater abundance, and more satisfaction. You'll live in the sweet spot of life without barriers to your visions and dreams. Breathe it in.

The *Quiet Mind* program is 100-percent natural. Altering your lifestyle and thoughts is free, the process is lean and clear, and requires no special education, resources, or infrastructure. When you change your brain, you change your health. Nurturing a quiet mind is your gradual progression back to your happiest, healthiest, and best self. This opportunity is your call to action as a self-empowered creator of your life. Now is the time to take ownership, to make the choices to make it happen. Do it for yourself and for those you love. When you raise your joy, you raise the joy of everyone around you.

Make sharing your experiences a part of your practice. Reach out, spread the word, network, be a leader, and support others. Join or start a resource group to reinforce your practice and motivate each other. It's our interpersonal dialogue that provides information, education, innovation, and dissolves stigma. It's those of us in the trenches who can generate the answers. It begins with a voice from all of us.

Be the master of your mind, not at the mercy of your mind. This is your gift of a predictable brain and stable life. With renewed self-confidence, your life will transform, and you can rise to your fullest potential. You are meant to live in joy. Come along. If I can do it, so can you.

From my heart to yours,

*Linda*

# About the Author

Linda Dierks is a pioneer in mental and physical wellness through personal power, the power of thought, and the power of love. Finding the source of wellness became her life's mission when breast cancer left her debilitated and depressed. After studying alternative health modalities, wellness philosophies, and cutting-edge research, she discovered the source of core healing and joy. Linda shares the methods behind her triumph over illness and depression as an author, teacher, radio host, and blogger.

# Connect with Linda

Linda's website: www.SpinStrawtoGoldNow.com

You can find Linda's radio programs at:
enlightenedworld.online.

Linda's Facebook page:
www.facebook.com/linda.dierks.75

Linda's Instagram: www.instagram.com/lindadierksvt

# Coming Soon

Find detailed information in Linda's upcoming book: *Three Stepping Stones to Wellness and Joy: A Woman, A Higher Presence, and Triumph Over Illness and Depression.*

# Disclaimer

Any and all information contained in Linda's website, blogs, programs, and books is for educational and informational purposes only and not intended to treat, cure, diagnose or intended to substitute for professional medical advice, diagnosis, or treatment from a trained medical professional who knows your detailed history. Some supplements can cause side effects. Always check with your medical doctor before starting any new program.

This information is made available to you as a self-help tool for your own use. Its role is to support and assist you in reaching your goals, but your success depends on your own effort, motivation, commitment, and follow-through. Linda cannot and does not guarantee that you will attain a particular result, and you accept and understand that results differ with each individual. Each individual's health and wellness success depends on his or her background, dedication, desire, and motivation.

.

Made in the USA
Columbia, SC
26 July 2019